Little Pieces of Light . . .
Darkness and Personal Growth

Joyce Rupp

Paulist Press
New York/Mahwah, New Jersey

The publisher gratefully acknowledges use of the following materials: Excerpt from *Care of the Soul* by Thomas Moore, copyright © 1992. Excerpt from *The Fruitful Darkness* by Joan Halifax, copyright © 1993. Excerpts from *When the Heart Waits* by Sue Monk Kidd, copyright © 1990. Excerpt from *A Tree Full of Angels* by Macrina Wiederkehr, copyright © 1988. All foregoing sources are reprinted by permission of HarperCollins Publishers. Poem by Caryll Houselander is used with permission of Christian Classics, Inc., Westminster, MD. Excerpts from *The Power of One* by Bryce Courtenay, copyright © 1989. Reprinted by permission of Random House, Inc. Excerpt from *Transitions* by William Bridges, copyright © 1980. Reprinted by permission of Addison-Wesley Publishing Co., Inc., Reading, MA. Excerpts from the *The New Jerusalem Bible*, copyright © 1985 by Darton, Longman & Todd, Ltd. and Doubleday, a division of Bantam Doubleday Dell Publishing Group, Inc. Reprinted by permission. Excerpt from *The Heroine's Journey* by Maureen Murdock. © 1990 by Maureen Murdock. Reprinted by arrangement with Shambhala Publications, Inc., 300 Massachusetts Avenue, Boston, MA 02115. Excerpt from *Gift of the Dark Angel: A Woman's Journey Through Depression Toward Wholeness* by Ann Keiffer. Copyright © 1991 by LuraMedia. Reprinted by permission of LuraMedia, Inc., San Diego, CA. Excerpts from the cassette tape set "Meeting God in Our Transition Times" by Joyce Rupp. Copyright © 1993 by Ave Maria Press. Used with permission of the publisher.

Cover/book design and interior illustrations by Nicholas T. Markell.

Copyright © 1994 by Joyce Rupp

Library of Congress Cataloging-in-Publication Data

Rupp, Joyce.
    Little pieces of light : darkness and personal growth / Joyce Rupp
        p.   cm. — (IlluminationBooks)
    ISBN 0-8091-3512-4 (pbk.)
    1. Suffering—Religious aspects—Christianity.   2. Consolation.
I. Title.   II. Series.
BV4909.R87   1994
248.8'6—dc20   94-30803
                                                                     CIP

Published by Paulist Press
997 Macarthur Boulevard
Mahwah, New Jersey 07430

Printed and bound in the
United States of America

Contents

Acknowledgments

Each time I write a book I am keenly aware of how I never do this by myself. It is both humbling and rewarding to remember how I have been influenced and guided by others' life experiences, expertise, and kindness.

I'm particularly grateful to my colleagues who shared their editing skills and their perspectives on ministry to those in darkness: hospital chaplain Carola Broderick, marriage and family therapist Nicola Hiatt Mendenhall, and pastor Thomas Pfeffer. I thank Betty Pomeroy from New York for her invitation to speak to the Eastern regional gathering of hospital chaplains. The seeds for this book took root in my preparation for that conference. My Boulder Hospice interfaith dialogue group, David Chernikoff, Lynn Bijili Marlow, Nora Smith and Diane Spearly, have given me constant support and insights. The gracious Benedictine women of St.

Walburga's Abbey in Boulder, Colorado have allowed me space and solitude in their guest house where I have studied and written. Robert Wicks of Loyola College in Maryland invited me to write this book—his encouragement has been greatly appreciated. My editor, Maria Maggi, has been a delightful source of support for me. Then, there are those many "little pieces of light in my life," all the people who have offered love, prayer, support to me—they are too numerous to mention all by name but they know that I know...and that I am deeply grateful. I especially thank my mother, Hilda Rupp, and Dorothy Sullivan, two women whose inner radiance has blessed my life.

Dedication

To:

my maternal grandmother
Cecelia Meyer Wilberding
who died in her 44th year
giving birth to her 13th child

IlluminationBooks
A Foreword

*I*lluminationBooks bring to light wonderful ideas, helpful information, and sound spirituality in concise, illustrative, readable, and eminently practical works on topics of current concern. Learning from stress; interior peace; personal prayer; biblical awareness; walking with others in darkness; appreciating the love already in our lives; spiritual discernment; uncovering helpful psychological antidotes for our tendency to worry too much at times; and important guides to improving interpersonal relations are only several of the areas which will be covered in this series.

The goal of each IlluminationBook then is to provide great ideas, helpful steps, and needed inspiration in small volumes. Each book offers a new beginning for the reader to explore possibilities and embrace practicalities which can be employed in everyday life.

In today's busy and anxious world, Illumination-Books are meant to provide a source of support—without requiring an inordinate amount of time or prior preparation. Each small work stands on its own. Hopefully, the information provided not only will be nourishing in itself but also will encourage further exploration in the area.

One is obviously never done learning. With every morsel of wisdom each of these books provides, the goal is to keep the process of seeking knowledge ongoing even during busy times when sitting down with a larger work is impossible or undesirable.

However, more than information (as valuable as it is), at the base of each work in the series is a deep sense of *hope* that is based on a belief in the beautiful statement made by Jesus to his disciples and in turn to us: "You are my friends." (Jn 15:15)

As "friends of God" we must seek the presence of the Lord in ourselves, in others, in silence and solitude, in nature, and in daily situations. IlluminationBooks are designed to provide implicit and explicit opportunities to appreciate this reality in new ways. So, it is in this Spirit that this book and the other ones in the series are offered to you.

—*Robert J. Wicks*
General Editor, IlluminationBooks

God will enter into your night,
as the ray of the sun enters
into the dark, hard earth,
driving right down
to the roots of the tree,
and there, unseen, unknown,
unfelt in the darkness,
filling the tree with life,
a sap of fire
will suddenly break out,
high above that darkness,
into living leaf and flame.
                    –*Caryll Houselander*

Introduction

One evening a group of us gathered for a Pipe Ceremony to ritualize and bring to a close our course on Native American spirituality. Our leader, a Yaqui Indian who had lived on a Lakota reservation, invited us to help prepare the classroom for the ceremony. He explained that the room, which had four windows, needed to be in total darkness. This space without light would symbolize the womb of Mother Earth from which we had all come. He told us that as we prayed during the Pipe Ceremony the blackened space would be a reminder to all of us that we were brothers and sisters, united as one in the Great Womb of Earth.

We set about the task of taping heavy black plastic garbage bags over all of the windows. We even taped over the door frame to make sure that all light would be eliminated from our space. Not one tiny crack or opening was to be left uncovered so that the room could be as womb-like as possible.

Finally, everything was tightly taped and we felt assured that, when the lights were switched off, the darkness desired for the ceremony would be complete. We sat down in our circle as our leader turned off the lights. At first we were met with an instant flood of blackness. I felt as if I had fallen into a dark hole in space. Then, as my eyes adjusted to the "hole," I saw these tiny little pieces of light. They were the wee sunbeams of a strong summer sun which had not yet set. These little pieces of light were penetrating infinitesimally small holes around the window frames which the tape had missed.

I smiled deeply inside myself as my life story stood up and took a bow. "Yes," I thought, "this is what has always sustained me in the tough times. No matter how thick the darkness, the light has remained. This reality has convinced me that I can live through dark experiences and not be overcome."

As I continued my ponderings during the Pipe Ceremony, I also gratefully recognized how darkness has become less of an enemy for me and more of a place of silent nurturance, where the slow, steady gestation needed for my soul's growth can occur. Not only is light a welcomed part of my life, but I am also developing a greater understanding of how much I need to befriend my inner darkness.

Darkness is a natural part of life but I have fought this reality for years. Darkness always seemed like a powerful intruder into my light-filled life. I had this notion that if I thought or did the right things then my life would always be full of light. I wouldn't have anguishing, dark times. Consequently, when the dark moments did come, I felt that something had gone terribly wrong with me. I presumed that I had failed in some significant way because I had not figured out how to keep the darkness out of my life. It has taken me a long time to recognize that darkness is an essential element for personal growth. No matter how many "right things" I do, darkness will still come unannounced and uninvited because it is an essential part of life. Without darkness I cannot become the person I am meant to be.

My acceptance of darkness as a help rather than a hindrance for growth has developed through both my life experiences and my studies. As I look back on my painful times, I see how much I have learned from the very situations that I wanted to immediately toss out of my life. I also see how the light is always there, perhaps totally hidden at times like the sun behind a heavy layer of clouds, but shining nonetheless.

I have listened to others tell their stories of dark journeys and have read numerous books and articles in

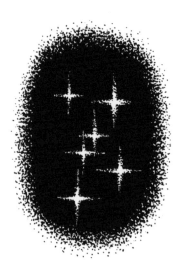

which the descent into the unknown regions of ourselves is considered a vital part of spiritual and psychological growth. All agree that we need light for our journey but we also need darkness. Perhaps only those who have suffered and struggled can fully understand and accept the truth of this paradoxical process of transformation.

In *Little Pieces of Light...Darkness and Personal Growth* I have written about darkness from various perspectives with the hope that you, the reader, will gain courage and hope. May you find comfort and guidance, whether you are in your own valley of darkness or are journeying with another who is experiencing a difficult time of trial. May the reality of darkness as an essential element of growth sustain you. May the power of the little pieces of light which penetrate the darkness give you reason to go on.

Chapter One
The Land of Darkness

t *he land of darkness, and shadow dark as death, where dimness and disorder hold sway, and light itself is like dead of night.*

◆ ◆ ◆

—Job 10:21-22 [1]

When I was training to be a Hospice volunteer, I had an unexpected experience which reminded me of how cutting and cruel darkness can be. One of our group exercises was meant to help us learn how someone with a terminal illness might feel. The facilitator gave each of us five small, square, white slips of paper. She asked us to think about what we most treasured in our life and to write one of these on each of the five pieces of paper. Then she told us to choose one of these treasures and to rip it up. I found this difficult to do. Next, we were told to choose another labeled paper and to tear this one up as well. I found that action even more difficult to do. Then our facilitator asked us to hold up the three remaining treasures. As we did so, she came to each one of us, picked out one of the papers, held it directly before our eyes, and ripped it up very matter-of-factly.

I'll never forget the moment she stood before me and took the one treasure I valued the most: "my spiritual life." Even though I knew that this was just an "activity," my heart felt a twinge of fear. Although I'd had numerous life experiences filled with darkness, in that moment I somehow knew with my whole being just what the darkness could actually demand of me.

Darkness comes in many forms and is not an easy visitor. Our life experiences when "dimness and disorder hold sway" are as many and as varied as we are. The Webster's Dictionary definition for darkness includes: "closed, hidden, not easily understood, obscure, gloomy, hopeless, entirely or partly without light." This description hardly touches the human experience of darkness. The darkness in the human heart also includes: lonely, shattered, dead, anxious, forlorn, bereft, despairing, discouraged, numbed, grief-laden, damaged, empty, bleak, fearful, traumatized, stumbling, aimless.

The land of darkness might be any or all of the following:

—a time in which the energy and focus of life is

almost completely funneled into physical, emotional, or pyschic pain

—an experience of being buried in deep sorrow and grief

—a discouraging and empty inner sojourn when nothing seems valuable or worthwhile

—a stage of spiritual desolation in which there is no sense of God's presence and little or no desire for things of the spirit

—a battle of indecision and struggle, when the unknowns and fears of the future press painfully upon decisions to be made

—a fog-like state when life is confusing, unclear, and seemingly impenetrable

—a situation with evil and atrocity which threatens to overpower or annihilate

—an excruciating time of helplessness in which one feels paralyzed or powerless to alleviate the pain of another

—an on-going siege of negativity which brings with it constant frustration, irritation and dissatisfaction

This list of general descriptions of darkness could go on and on. Some people experience constant forms of darkness and others have only occasional bouts when the "light itself is like dead of night." No one can say whose darkness is the greatest but everyone experiences some form of darkness from time to time. Like Job, we all long to have life return to the way it used to be, or the way that we have longed for it to be.

One of the most common labels which many give to darkness is that of "depression." Yet, even depression comes in as many different forms as there are people. For some, this darkness is a life-long, never-ending valley of despair and thoughts of self-destruction. For others, it is a sporadic greyness that chills happiness and leaves the spirit blah. And yet for others, depression consists of foul moods with emotions such as anger, self-pity, guilt, sadness, bitterness, or apathy, which pull one down and hack away at a positive attitude. Whatever form depression takes, it has a Job-like quality and most often reeks with loss of self-esteem and deceptive mind-messages about who we are and the way life is.

Sometimes darkness can develop when we are facing something unknown in our lives. It may come as we search for the missing pieces of truth about the past. Illness can have its share of unknowns, too, especially when the illness is difficult to diagnose or is terminal. Questions about the future can also contribute to one's darkness as well as all those life events which disrupt and shatter our hopes and dreams, or deprive us of anyone or anything which we value and hold dear.

Darkness can also break into our inner world when we experience the natural patterns of adult growth such as midlife, retirement, and other aging processes. At these times, darkness challenges us to peer into our Shadow and to accept parts of our selves which we have not known, have refused to acknowledge, or have skillfully hidden from ourselves.

Life can go along well for us for a long time and then, suddenly, ker-plunk, into the darkness we go. A member of a religious community in her 80's shared with me that she did not have any difficulty accepting the aging process until her 80th birthday. Then, unexpectedly, she plunged into the depths of darkness in a way she had never known before. It was a call to directly face her own mortality which left her feeling vulnerable, insecure, and helpless. Until this time of her life, she had been able to brush aside the whispers of death and the questions of what lies beyond this side of life.

Sometimes the land of darkness is a spiritual wasteland which is commonly referred to as "the dark night of the soul," a term used by the mystic, John of the Cross. When the "dark night" comes it can be quite terrifying because it seems one has lost the last link with hope: a relationship with God. The voice of the soul cries out in utter abandonment: "Where do I go when the deepest Source of guidance and comfort is apparently no longer with me?" Often accompanying this sense of total loss is the added torment of recognizing our flaws and failures more clearly than ever before.

The violence and destruction happening in the world can also bring darkness. Discouragement and desolation can easily find those who open their hearts to people who have been victims of atrocities and abuse. The realization of collective evil can fall like a heavy, black cloud upon the person who cares about what happens in this world. When anyone accompanies another's pain with compassion, there's bound to be a taste of darkness.

In spite of all the pain and agony that darkness brings, these periods of sparse light in our lives can also be gifts for our growth. We can never live for very long without some dark moments pushing their way into our days. This is life's way of inviting us to grow. Whether or not the darkness is a gift for us depends, of course, upon our attitude toward it and how we respond.

We need the darkness for our spiritual and psychological health but this is a painful truth to accept. It's extremely difficult to believe this when we are feeling depressed. I've yet to hear anyone say, "Oh, I am so grateful. I woke up this morning feeling so wretched and depressed. I know it's a good sign that I am in another stage of growth. I can't wait until this darkness deepens some more."

Darkness can be helpful and transforming if we are willing to stay open to it. Thomas Moore writes:

> The Greeks tell the story of the minotaur, the bull-headed flesh eating man who lived in the center of the labyrinth. He was a threatening beast, and yet his name was Asterion—Star. I often think of this paradox as I sit with someone with tears in her eyes, searching for some way to deal with a death, a divorce, or a depression. It is a beast, this

thing that stirs in the core of her being, but it is also the star of her innermost nature.[2]

When the terrible flooding of 1993 happened in the Midwest, a seventy-five year old woman described how she sat, watching the river rise around her home. She said it was the longest day of her life. During the flooding, her neighbors all joined together to protect her house with sandbags. They reached out to each other in ways they had never done before. She described how one of them, whom everyone talked about as the local prostitute, was the most concerned and helpful during this treacherous time. This older woman had never known her neighbor very well but she welcomed the care and kindness which this supposed prostitute offered to her. The danger of Asterion in the flooding brought them together. The star of Asterion gave them a deeper respect for one another as loving humans who needed each other in a dark time.

There is no way that we can avoid inner darkness completely. If we did so, we would be tossing out a vital part of our transformation. Rather than getting rid of darkness, we need to search for ways that we can befriend it. Joan Halifax writes:

> ...we cannot eliminate the so-called negative forces of afflictive emotions. The only way to work with them is to encounter them directly, enter their world and transform them. They then become

manifestations of wisdom. Our weaknesses become our strengths, the source of our compassion for others and the basis of our awakened nature.[3]

Does this mean that we should allow any and all kinds of abusive behavior, continue accepting addictive situations, wallow in meaningless depression, give in to an apathetic attitude of not caring what happens, or simply live with relationships that have gone sour and died? No, of course not. Yet, in the midst of this darkness, which we must bear until the situation can be changed, is the fertilizer of our soul's growth.

The difficult thing about darkness as an essential part of life is that we can know this fact intellectually but run from it emotionally. All we care about is getting rid of the dreadful experience, moving on, feeling good again. When darkness descends upon the human heart, we spend most of our energy doing battle with it rather than befriending it and seeing what gift (what "star") it might be offering to us.

Any kind of darkness can call us, push us, nudge us, and urge us onto the path of inner growth. Darkness can wake us up and stir questions in us that we'd rather not face:

How do the patterns of my behavior influence my life?

Whom or what have I taken for granted?

Have I been attentive to the deepest longings of my soul?

What do I really want to do with my life?

How will I make choices for the future?

Whom do I want to be with me as I continue my life journey?

Out of these deep, stirring questions of darkness, we can be led to clearer awareness regarding our strengths and weaknesses. They can give us a new vision about "the way life is," helping us to discover greater inner freedom to be who we are meant to be. The questions of darkness can gift us with a willingness to live with insecurity and to find deeper joy in the things of life we so easily assume will always be there for us.

In a sense, the darkness forces us inward. We can try to sit the darkness out, or withdraw into ourselves, or get completely absorbed in life's constant pressure of activities. A much more healthy and growthful option is to be open to the darkness that is present, listen to it, hear what it has to say, rather than trying to just survive with it or attempt to boot it out the door as quickly as possible.

Even though we must accept and befriend darkness as a part of the cycle of growth, we must not totally give in to it. This is one of the major paradoxes of personal growth. Accepting and befriending darkness is like allowing someone to live in our house for a while but being very emphatic and clear that this is only a visit and not a permanent residence. We cannot give all of our time and concern to the darkness even though this visitor wants to take up all the space in our house.

We cannot simply withdraw and give all of our

resources to darkness. We must hold our own ground, stand up to darkness, and not let this visitor push us around. If we allow darkness to take over our dwelling completely it can be extremely harmful and dangerous, rather than growthful, for us.

This takes extreme effort at times because we feel the tremendous power which darkness can exert over us. So we go to others, like ministers, therapists, spiritual directors, good friends, caring physicians, wise persons who can help us with the delicate balance of befriending darkness yet also keeping a healthy distance. This balance is never easy to achieve and with each visit of darkness we have to learn the process all over again.

As we walk with the land of darkness in our hearts, there are two truths which must be consistently held close to our hearts. The first is that darkness can be an opportunity for growth. Secondly, a day will come when the darkness will dissipate and the light will take over again. We do not have to sit on the Job-like dung heap of darkness forever but we must accept a place on it for a while.

Prayer

O God,
I have been to my inner place
where shadows are as dark as death.

I have been to the land of gloom
where my security shudders
and my dreams are coffined.

I want to believe and trust
that this land of desolation
contains a gift of growth for me.

Convince me. Assure me it is so.

Wrap this truth of transformation
firmly around my questioning heart.
                    –Joyce Rupp

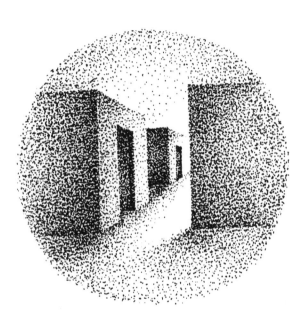

Chapter Two
Leave the Hall Light On

*T*oo many of us panic in the dark. We don't understand that it's a holy dark and that the idea is to surrender to it and journey through to real light.[4]

                                                  –Sue Monk Kidd

      Fear was the hidden message that I heard in a conversation between a small boy and his father. It was part of a televison commercial urging parents to vaccinate their children as a prevention for childhood diseases. The television screen was completely black as the young boy, obviously in bed, called out to his father: "Dad, would you check the closet again?" "Are you sure there's no one under the bed?" The father kept reassuring him that nothing and no one was there. Finally, the two voices said goodnight to each other. There was a pause and then the tiny voice pleaded: "Dad, could you leave the hall light on?" Immediately following this typical evening conversation between a parent and child, an adult voice was heard: "There are some things you *should* be afraid of," with a message on the TV screen about where to seek vaccinations for children.

My heart leaned into this conversation for several reasons. I remembered my own childhood fear of the dark and how all those imaginary sounds and shapes seemed like real persons and monsters to me. I also thought of how fear of the dark is not limited to childhood. It just changes direction as we move into adulthood. Instead of being afraid of the darkness *outside* of us, we focus our fear as adults on the darkness *inside* of us.

I also resonated with the voice saying that there are some things that we definitely need to fear. We do need a healthy fear of dangerous darkness so that we can be protected from what seeks to maim, wound, or destroy us. There is a darkness that can consume people, gobble their minds and suck out their spirits. There are mentally ill patients whose battle never ends and highly resentful, angry or bitter persons who refuse to be healed. Dangerous darkness also lurks in situations where abuse, torture, or the destruction of another's life takes place. Wherever there is intimidation or a brutal taking away of life in any form, there is a dangerous darkness.

Much of what we fear, however, is not so much a

dangerous darkness as a "holy dark," the kind of darkness we just don't want to have but which is essential for our growth. It stands in the way of our comfortableness, our convenience, our familiarity, our security, our desire for control and our need to "have it all together." This "holy dark" consists of those life opportunities which bring gloom, struggle, and depression. They feel like a curse but are really a blessing. These "holy dark" experiences bear the touch of God's grace and wait to transform us if only we will open up to their gifts.

The emotions associated with darkness are the ones we often experience in times of grief because in the darkness we tend to feel as though we've lost a part of ourselves. Anger surfaces as we rage against the darkness, or we feel overwhelmed, or get on our pity-pots, or withdraw, hide out, or avoid life. We can feel confused, irritable, restless, or be in a constant state of running in an effort to escape the perpetually grim days.

Darkness can be caused by grieving the loss of someone we love or it can bear the marks of grief itself because it feels as if a part of ourselves has died, and maybe it has. Maybe this part had to die, or get out of the way, or be lost for a while so that another part of us could be uncovered or given due attention. We long to retrieve this lost part of us that is hidden in the gloom or dying on the roadside of our pain. At the same time, another part of us is waiting to be discovered, crying out: "Look at me! Listen to me! I long to be embraced by you!" but we refuse to hear what it has to say to us because we are so absorbed in the emotions which accompany our darkness.

I met a woman at a retreat who told me the story of her deep and long journey of darkness. It began when she was forced to retire from a teaching position at a university because of her age. She described how unfair she felt this was because she still had much energy and vitality. Depression, anger, and alienation wrapped themselves around her heart. Fear took over and she was certain that she would have nothing more to offer to others, that her gifts and enthusiasm would turn to ashes. She allowed this fear to dominate her moods and behavior as she withdrew from people and activities.

After being in this hostile, dark world for over two years, the pastor of her local parish invited her to a meeting in which he spoke about the great need of visitors to care for the older, disabled, shut-in members of the parish. Fearfully and hesitantly, she began to do this work. To her amazement, she enjoyed the new challenge and, as she told me, "I love this work more than anything I've ever done in my life." Only when she "lost" the teaching part of herself did the pastoral, compassionate part of herself rise up and make itself known.

Fear has a way of shoving its way through our security and our intelligence and all the wisdoms we've learned. This emotion wheedles its way into our mind and convinces us of all sorts of untruths. Fear can misdirect our path and lead us astray with its spooky voice and false suggestions. As Bryce Courtenay writes in *The Power of*

One: "The imagination is always the best torturer."[5] Fear of the unknown or of the consequences of the darkness can play a major role in our imagination. Fear torments us with questions and shows us imaginary monsters of the future. Doubts and haunting questions rise up in us and threaten to choke our hope: "Will this ever end? Am I doing the right thing? Will I find my way out of this maze? Will I ever trust another person? Can I open myself to love again? Will I be able to adapt to my changed body?" When I allow fear to take over my imagination, I often believe that the darkness will overpower me and that I will not find my balance. I fear that I will be beaten down forever, that I will always feel lonely, desolate, empty, and energyless, and that I will never regain my taste for joy and beauty.

Carol Pregent described her wrestling with darkness and the fear of never having her life together again in this way:

> I feel fragmented, broken in pieces like a puzzle all spread out on the table. None of the pieces are together and I am not even sure if they will fit together. There are so many pieces that I fear I will not be able to put them back together. Is it an insurmountable task?[6]

Sometimes fear rises up in us and actually brings on the darkness. Anxiety can descend when enormous risks come or when a child will soon leave home for adult life. Apprehension may loom large when the great gap that's developed in a relationship becomes more and more apparent or when aging parents become terribly frail and fragile. A quiet dread may be present when some haunting and unwanted truth begins to call to us from the depths of our beings.

What can we do about our fear of the darkness? The first thing is to accept it as a natural response to both inner and outer darkness. It is to be expected. Stephen Levine tells the story of how an old man, a great Tibetan saint, was meditating one day when three dark figures came to his cave. They were "rattling skulls and bloody swords, shrieking obscenities and exuding the smell of rotten flesh." The great saint looked up, gave them a smile and invited them to "take tea." The dark figures were amazed that he was not terrified. The old man replied that he was grateful to be on the path of healing and that their ugliness only reminded him "to be aware and have mercy."[7]

It is helpful to remember that most fears are never realized. They rarely actually happen. They are bullying Goliaths, pushing the little David in us around, trying to paralyze us with inaction so that we do not grow into the person we are meant to be. Our fears try to keep us in our place. A good friend cured me of a lot of my anxiety by always asking me in my dark times: "What's the worst possible thing that could happen? Then, "How probable is this?" It was always a good reality check for me and helped me to put some distance between my fear and what was actually happening. By taking a close look at what is real, factual, and what is from the imagination, we can lessen the power that fear has over us.

We need to face our fears in our dark times. These fears take a lot of energy from us when they are ignored or denied. Our fears can dominate our lives and leave us stress-filled all the time. In Ursula LeGuin's Earth/Sea Trilogy, the main character, Ged, was terrified by a dark thing that kept chasing him. He ran and ran and ran from this dark shadow of a thing. The faster he ran from this dark form the faster it ran after him. Finally, Ged could run no more. He was exhausted and exasperated. In a whirl of desperation, he turned around and faced the huge dark thing. At that precise moment, when he faced this looming figure, it turned around and ran for its life.

A similar, real-life story is that of a woman who was brutally raped. She continued to be psychologically traumatized by her rapist even after he was convicted of the crime. She lived in terror and suspicion all the time. Finally, when she reached a near breaking point, she made a decision to visit him at the county jail. She confronted him with her anger and demanded an apology from him. He never gave her an apology but choosing to see him face to face gave her back her power and she broke the strong hold that the darkness of the rape had on her.[8]

So it is with our worst fears; they must be faced: "What is it that scares me so much?" We must turn around and look at it, whether that fear is named loneliness, vulnerability, illness, failure, dying, joblessness, lack of identity, rejection, loss of faith, or any other thing that terrorizes our heart and mind. I've learned that when I turn around and look at my fear it never carries the immense power that it first had over me. I may shudder and shake when I meet it, but I also know that it does not have to conquer me unless I allow it to do so. The more I believe that darkness is essential for my personal growth, the less power fear will have over me.

While it is essential to turn around and face my fear, I must also learn how to discipline my mind so that I dwell on other things besides my fear. I cannot ignore the fear but I also cannot allow it to hang around and torment me all day. I can "have tea" with my fear but then I send fear on its way. I find that it helps to talk about my fear with a safe person or group. As I say my fear out loud it gets smaller and I get stronger. I can also feel comfort by knowing that others understand my fears and may well have had similar ones. Finally, it's a bit pun-ny but I also need to "lighten up" when I am in darkness. How easy it is to toss aside my sense of humor when life is bleak. Yet, this is when I most need to laugh.

It does become easier to live in the darkness the more we can see that this phase of our lives is just that, a phase, a necessary part of our humanity, and that eventually it will pass. A colleague of mine once asked me if the pain and turmoil he was experiencing ever ceased. Much later in life, when he had been through the darkness, he told me: "The one thing that I kept clinging to and which gave me hope was when you answered my question "Does it get better?" with "Yes, it does. It may take a while but it does get better."

This darkness will lessen. I must believe this. But I must also accept that I will never be exactly the same as I was before the darkness. This life event or situation will affect my life. This is another reason for opening up to change. At the moment it seems it can only be a negative change but there will be surprising positive developments if I am willing to receive them.

As I face my fear, I do need a "hall light on." I need the assurance that there's a way out of all this mess eventually, and that someone's there who will offer comfort and support as I wait in the darkness. Sometimes my "hall light" has been another person who never gave up on me. Sometimes my only "hall light" has been God. When darkness was extremely private or unnamed, I could only find solace in the One whom I knew would never let me go. I have often taken comfort in Psalm 23: "Even though I walk through the darkest valley, I fear no evil; for you are with me."⁹ I am always assured by the stories from Scripture, all those women and men who had tough times, because God continually gives two messages over and over to those in darkness: "Do not fear" and "I am with you." I find great comfort in these assurances and clutch them to my empty heart when times are tough.

Prayer

O God,
I am afraid in the darkness.
I pull the sheets of security around me
and view all my imaginings with terror.

These fears rise up in the shadows of my soul,
like wild warriors ready to attack me.

Though I hide from these monsters of my making,
or attempt to flee on the road of anxiety,
they are always pursuing, close behind me.

Help me to turn around and face my fears.
Do not let them have power over me.
May I not succumb to the terrors of my mind
which chase me relentlessly in the darkness.

–Joyce Rupp

Chapter Three
Silent Stirrings in the Tomb

*B*ut I shall be wise this time and wait
in the dark...[10]

–Rabindranath Tagore

I like to envision myself outside the emptied Easter
tomb, sitting there with the joyful angel, or marveling with
the surprised Mary as she hurries away to announce the
good news of resurrection. But the thought of being inside
that airless, eerie tomb with its dark, damp smell of death
does not entice me one bit. My strong inclination toward
light bids me ignore Holy Saturday, the day of "in
between." The part of me that resists waiting hides from
the unknown and the uncontrolled. Resurrection, with its
abundant, vibrant life, appeals to me. I'd much rather for-

get that the Easter tomb was once occupied or that the tiny green bud on the bush was once encased in ice and snow. In the same way, I tend to forget that the wisdom I've come to know was once dormant in the dim corridors of myself.

I wonder if it might not be this way for most people. Christians tend to ignore this "day of in between" with their ritual focused on Good Friday and on the celebration of Easter. Whatever happened to the significant symbolic event of time in the tomb? This part of the story which is absolutely essential is the very one that is most likely to be ignored, set aside, or forgotten. Yet, the dark waiting is vital to the story. There is no Easter until the tomb has a resident for a while.

Every moment of resurrection, whether of the earth or of the human heart, contains its own "Holy Saturday" when the darkness smells of death and the tomb shows no evidence of life. It is during this tomb time that life stirs, moves, and changes into something surprising. It is here in the tomb or the cave "that Jung says a person goes when there is a great work to be accomplished, an effort from which one recoils."[11]

It is easy to sound poetic or idealistic when writing about the tomb time. Darkness is certainly not this way. Just ask someone who is languishing in memories of a loved one who's died, or someone who is excruciatingly ill, or despairing to the point of contemplating suicide, or desperately clutching at the last bits of self-worth. These people know that darkness is not just some charming companion who comes along and says, "Join me. I have some truth for you."

This place of "in between" is filled with agonizing silence and painful hollowness. It has been described with various images throughout the years: tomb, underworld, womb, cave, desert, chrysalis—they all bear the same mark: they are the dark waiting rooms of transformation. William Bridges uses the term "neutral zone" to characterize this seemingly unproductive stage of growth:

> We aren't sure what is happening to us or when it will be over. We don't know whether we are going crazy or becoming enlightened.... For many people the experience of the neutral zone is essentially one of emptiness in which the old reality looks transparent and nothing feels solid anymore"[12]

I thought about all this as I went walking one Holy Saturday on a hiking trail which I had just discovered in the foothills of the Rockies. The trail meandered through a canyon, along a narrow, lively, recently melted creek. Spring was evident everywhere in the fresh green of the earth. What particularly caught my eye were the tiny, ripe buds of bushes and grasses. I'd never looked so closely at buds to see what a variety of hues they possessed: magenta, lime green, brown, orange, tan, red and deep purple. They seemed to call to me with some significant message so I stood there for a long while and waited for them to speak to me.

As I stood and waited, I began to marvel at the power of life which had pushed the buds toward such ripeness. I thought of how they had patiently waited, waited, waited, for the right moment before they could come forth from their wintered tomb. It was then that I heard the message they were offering to me: it is in the neutral zone time, the winter season of the heart, when all seems dead and barren that the potential for life is being nurtured and readied for the hurrah of Springtime. In the Winter, who would believe that the empty branches of those bushes would ever sing with sweet green again? In the tomb time of our lives, who of us would ever believe that our hearts would be singing again with the sweet sounds of joy and enthusiasm?

There's a power in the plant that fills the buds and responds to the warmth of the sun and the moisture pushing up from the roots. It is like the power of the Eastered tomb when the linens fell off and the Risen One danced out into the golden glow of morning. It is the power of the Radiant Light in us, urging us to stay in the struggle, to wait in the dark, to believe in the value of the tomb stage of our journey, and to trust that our own bud time will come again.

Having to wait and wait and wait without answers, or direction, or an easing of the emptiness, can cause such anxiety in the dark of the tomb. Eastering can't be rushed or forced and there are no clocks or calendars telling us when resurrection is going to happen. No baby in the womb has ever had a map that said "this way out."

The child has to wait until the push of the contractions thrusts the womb door open. No seed in the soil has a sign that says "this way up." No, the seed just waits until the warmth penetrates the soil and draws the first sheath of green from beyond the broken-open shell. No butterfly developing in the chrysalis has a schedule and a timetable posted next to her. No, she just waits and gives herself to the unfolding process. Jesus, too, had to wait until the angels came and unbound him from the burial shroud. ("They took him down from a tree and buried him in a tomb. But God raised him from the dead" Acts 13:26-27).

Maureen Murdock has written about this struggle in her tomb-like description of the descent to the underworld:

> In the underworld there is no sense of time; time is endless and you cannot rush your stay.... This all-pervasive blackness is moist, cold, and bone-chilling. There are no easy answers in the underworld; there is no quick way out. Silence pervades when the wailing ceases. One is naked and walks on the bones of the dead.[13]

When we plant a seed in the soil or when a caterpillar spins a cocoon there's no way of telling what's going on inside or exactly how long the wait is going to be. We can't dig up the seed to check and see if there's growth or slip open the cocoon and peer inside because this would cause death. We can't peer into the tomb of

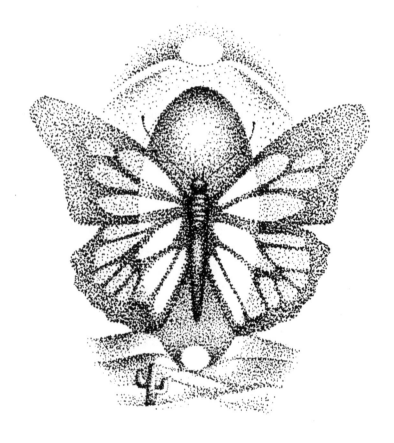

our self and see if something is stirring in there either. It's truly a journey of trust in the transformative process. All kinds of inner stirrings are going on but we simply cannot see them taking place. We must trust that the greening and the growing needed for our life's journey is happening without our being able to see it.

I recall a time when I was speaking with a group and I used the example of how the little creature in a chrysalis just hangs and hangs there while all sorts of phenomenal changes are going on. I asked them: "Who would ever believe that a monarch butterfly would come forth from that dark brown sack?" Just then one of the participants spoke up and said, "Yeah, well it's easy for that creature. But me? When I'm in my dark time, I can't just hang there and wait to be born. I have to shower, grocery shop, care for my children, get to work, etc." She was right but the reality remains: we cannot hurry the "in between" time and we cannot know in the womb of our darkness what our growth will look like when we eventually resurrect.

There is a subtle suggestion in many resources and therapeutic curatives today which claims "if you just read this, do this, exerience this...then the darkness will quickly vanish." This approach implies that "if you think the right things, give yourself the correct messages, etc." you won't have any darkness in your life. This voice is a false one and can actually detain or stall our journey of growth because all light and no darkness is not the way that transformation occurs.

A good book or an insight from someone or a positive mental image or message can sustain us or point us in the right direction of our growth but we still have to contend with the waiting period of darkness. Good therapists, ongoing support groups, deep meditation, healing music, or energizing workshops can guide, console, comfort, or free us as we go through the darkness but they won't make the darkness disappear. When darkness seems to "instantly vanish" or never be a part of our lives, it is usually being repressed or denied and will make a return appearance at a later unnamed time and place. We can do all the "right things" but sooner or later we have to live for a while in that tomb-like experience of waiting and wondering if the light will ever reappear.

It always seems quite amazing to me how readily nature accepts this dark passageway of life. Snakes shed their skin, birch trees say goodbye to their bark, lobsters leave their shells behind at least seven times, caterpillars spin their own dark homes and polar bears crawl into their caves of hibernation for a long season of inactivity. But we humans scream out against this "leaving behind" and "letting go." Sitting in the darkness and waiting doesn't come naturally for us even though we "sat" for nine months in our mother's womb, a development which is as mysterious and marvelous as that of a caterpillar metamorphosizing into a butterfly.

The Hebrew Scriptures tell the story of the people who hurried out of Egypt's slavery and traveled for years and years in an unknown land of wilderness. These people thought that they were just wandering around, directionless, lost and empty, but they were actually wending their way to the "promised land." As they did so, they were learning all sorts of things about their faith, their insecurities, their strengths and their weaknessses. It was during this long sojourn that the people of the Exodus story discovered the immense power of God's faithful love and the resilience of their own spirits. It was only when they came to the promised land of Canaan and looked back at their wanderings that they truly understood the effects of their desert experience.

Jesus recognized the necessity of going through the "in between" time long before he went through it in his own passion and death. He urged his followers to be willing to let go or to die to self in order to be more fully alive. But messages like "lose your life to find it" and "the grain of wheat has to fall into the ground and die or it stays just a grain of wheat" are often lost in the fear of having to spend some time in the dark waiting room of letting go (Lk 9:24; Jn 12:24). Certain parts of us have to change radically if we are going to grow.

This changing happens in those dark times of the unknown when we have little to which we can cling and a lot to surrender. The cross has to be carried, the old self has to be shed. This journey requires a tremendous amount of letting go and "dying" to what gives comfort and security. Thus, it brings with it some inherent anxiety.

In the Roman Catholic Eucharistic Canon the celebrant prays that the congregation will be "freed from all anxiety." I used to think that this plea was a rather ridiculous, inhuman concept. As I have grown in understanding the necessity for darkness as a part of the journey of growth, I see the wisdom of this prayer. It may seem to be an impossibility for the human heart to be freed from all anxiety but it is the goal of one who truly accepts the value of waiting in the womb of growth. The more I am convinced of this value, the less I need to fret and worry as I usually do when the dark times come. Trust in the process of transformation is a giant leap and it takes a lifetime to do. I must be patient with myself and with the process.

Some people have learned this lesson of transformation well. I heard someone who'd seen more than his share of life's adversities remark: "Well, what do you expect? You can't do a long jump and not expect to get some sand in your shorts." After I quit laughing I remember thinking to myself how much I needed to have more of that kind of attitude. I want life to be neat, clean and tidy, not messy, disruptive, confusing and irritating. But this is not the way it works. Whether the darkness comes from the external events of my life or from some inner call that bids me go deeper, it can lead to much greater personal freedom to be my true self.

We always need to have a balance—to enter freely into the waiting room of darkness and yet to not gorge ourselves on the pain and discomfort of this. We have all met people who wear their woes, worries, and old hurts like a breastplate of self-esteem. It's their way of drawing attention to themselves, of deriving some long-sought human care and compassion, or meeting some other deep need within themselves.

The stirrings in the tomb of our darkness are the whispers of our soul, urging us to move toward a place where we have not been before. We may be pushed to make changes in our lives that we would never have considered otherwise. We may be forced to look at hidden wounds and inner issues that we had always been able to shove aside. We may be led to appreciate life and our gifts at a much deeper level. Most always, the womb of darkness is a catalyst for creativity and for a deeper relationship with God. Always it is a time for trust in the transformative process and for faith that something worthwhile is to be gained by our waiting in the dark.

Prayer

O God,
I wait in the unending darkness
like a chrysalis on a lonely limb.

I am living in the dreadful "in between"
of death and life, of darkness and light,
not coming, not going, just hanging on.

I fight the seeming emptiness
and struggle against required surrender.

Teach me to wait patiently,
while my wings grow strong,
for my time to fly has not yet come.

–Joyce Rupp

Chapter Four
Separate Bedrooms

I *know what it feels like to want God like I want my own breath. I know what it feels like to experience nothing but darkness and silence.*[14]

–Macrina Wiederkehr

We were sitting in a circle as we opened the retreat on transitions. I asked the group to share their name and one thing about themselves that they wanted the group to know about them. When it came time for a petite, thirty-five year old woman to speak, she gave her name and said, "If I were to describe my relationship with God, I'd say it was like separate bedrooms."

Her unexpected, surprising remark was met by

laughter and then by a compassionate, somber silence as she described her anger and despair when she recently learned that her cancer had reoccurred for the third time. She was "angry as hell" at God and felt that coming to the retreat was the last thing she should probably be doing. "In fact," she said, "I may not even stay for this whole thing."

What this despondent woman was experiencing is not unusual. Our life with God is bound to be affected when all the other parts of our life are in the wilderness. We cannot isolate our spiritual life and "freeze it" in a perpetual state of happiness while the rest of our life mourns and thrashes in the valley of darkness.

As a spiritual director who has traveled the dark journey myself as well as with others, I have found some common responses, or natural consequences, which happen in our spiritual life. Once in a while, a person in great darkness continues to feel a strong bond with God. In fact, it is the one thing that gets them through the desolate journey. But for most, this is not so. Usually people in darkness experience a vast chasm between themselves and God. No matter how they try to pray or worship, God seems hidden and unavailable.

Often when we try to pray in the dark stage of transformation, our prayer feels like dry sawdust. We have absolutely no felt experience of God's nearness. Our spiritual life seems empty and barren and we leave our time of prayer wondering if it has been worth the effort. Oftentimes this leads to boredom and a "who cares" attitude. Sometimes there is a total lack of desire to pray. Our head says "You ought to be trying to stay connected with God" but the rest of us fights the doing of it. Prayer seems futile or useless.

During this time, there's usually a strong restlessness when we attempt to pray. We can't concentrate or sit still for very long. It can be an excruciating time in which we feel as though we've failed miserably in our efforts.

Questions about God's nearness or presence arise. We may feel as though we've been abandoned by the One whom we thought would never leave us. We ask ourselves whatever happened to all those glorious promises of God in the scriptures which assured us: "I will be with you." Anger at God can easily push its way through as we feel this abandonment.

We can get very impatient with God or with ourselves. We expect so much and so little is happening. Our mind keeps badgering us with thoughts like: "If I'm being faithful to my spiritual life, why don't I feel any better?" "How long will this go on?" "Will I ever feel God's nearness again?"

Along with this, guilt makes its way into our darkness. Little messages creep into our discomfort like: "I should be able to pray." "Maybe if I just prayed longer." "I ought to feel better about this. I must be doing something wrong." We start to doubt our choice of prayer and look for other ways to pray, thinking that this might change things.

Our perception of who God is to us is often challenged during a time of darkness. How often I hear comments like: "I don't know *whom* to pray to anymore." We seem unable to name God and we don't know what we can expect from this God. This confusion adds to our sense of distancing from God and makes it even tougher to stay connected.

When there is great despair or depression in the darkness, one can also struggle with thoughts of suicide. During this time, we give up all hope of God's being with us and of the burden of darkness being lifted from us. Prayer becomes less a rage against the darkness and more a total and complete withdrawal from both self and God.

An unyielding wall of separation from God normally develops when our darkness is deep and persistent. It is challenging to believe that this, too, can be a part of our personal growth. Yet, there are numerous ways in which the darkest moments of our spiritual life are teaching us and guiding us to new vision and deeper living. We must keep searching in our dark times because that is the place where we are to learn something about our relationship with God:

> I hauled my depression from sanctuary to sanctuary, but found no sanctuary. I was a spiritual misfit and went away all the more depressed that I could not embrace these churches or feel embraced by them. Maybe I'd come to a bad time, and God wasn't in right then. Actually, God was

in. In the place I hadn't looked yet: in the depths of depression.[15]

God may well be inviting us to reconsider just whom we perceive God to be. What we believe about God always has an effect on our life but particularly when we are going through a dark time. If we believe that God got us into this mess, or if we believe that we've done something wrong and we are being punished for it, or if we see God as some sort of "instant fixer of all ills," we will fall more deeply into the hole of darkness.

Our understanding and our metaphors for God may be too limiting for our adult life. Perhaps we need to be stretched into considering God as the dark God of the womb as well as the God of light. Maybe we need to move beyond the God who judges us to the God who loves us totally, without any reservations. It may be that we are being challenged to welcome the feminine qualities of God as well as the masculine ones. Our beliefs about God are as difficult to let go of as anything else in our life. It is not easy to welcome an aspect of the Divine that calls us beyond where we now are.

The darkness may also provide an opportunity for us to look at our weaknesses which we have heretofore avoided. Recognition of our own sinfulness can bring us into greater clarity and depth about our humble dependence on the power of God to transform us. It was during an extended retreat that I first recognized my inner possibilities for evil. It was an overwhelming time of dark-

ness for me as I named this part of myself. However, the truths I learned during this experience have been some of my greatest gifts. They have helped me become a much more open, non-judgmental listener to the faults and failings of others. These truths have also helped me to extend greater compassion and understanding toward my own person now that I know I can't manage my struggle for goodness all by myself.

Whenever I go through a time of darkness, I almost always feel called to let go of something and to accept being out of control in some way. I fight this but eventually I see how I am not the sole manager of my spiritual journey. There are parts of me that need to be surrendered to God. My ego, or my "I," wants so much and keeps a tough hold on me so that I am not free to grow in the ways which are necessary for my growth. Sometimes it takes the vulnerable and defenseless posture of darkness to squeeze loose my strong grasp on my ideas or my secure ways of living.

I remember seeing a foreign film when I was in my twenties. It was titled: "The World of Apu." The only piece of this film that I can remember is one that astounded me then, and still does today. Apu had written reams of paper about his concepts and life experiences. At a certain point in his life, he went through a deep and long depression. At the end of this era of emptiness, Apu is seen sitting on a high hill with all the reams of paper in his lap. He very deliberately tosses all of the papers to the wind and they are carried away from him forever.

This profound gesture of letting go gave him the freedom he needed to move on with his life.

In my youth I thought that it was absolutely crazy to toss those papers to the wind. As an older adult, I still think it was a bit crazy to do that, but I now see that there is no other way except to do it if I am to continue to grow. Surrender to God is an essential part of growth on the spiritual journey and sometimes it demands my letting go of what is held most closely to my heart.

Being able to let go and let God take over one's life demands a tremendous amount of trust in this Divine Companion. Thomas Merton writes that "true love and prayer are really learned in the hour when prayer becomes impossible and your heart turns to stone."[16] It is in the hour of our greatest darkness that we discover that we are never truly alone. It is the time when we learn to trust that God's love is so much more than we ever imagined. We learn to trust that God sits there with us in our shadow of death even though we cannot touch this Presence with our human longings.

> When we enter the spiritual night, we can feel alone, encompassed by a fearful darkness. What we need to remember is that we're carried in God's womb, in God's divine heart, even when we don't know it, even when God seems far away.[17]

I finally learned this when I was in the hospital for my first experience of major surgery. I had no idea of how wretched and helpless I would feel when I first came out of surgery. As I gradually came out of the anesthetic and felt the pain, I looked over and saw a friend who was a member of my community sitting there in the corner of the room. She was so kind to me that day and stayed with me through the entire day. I knew that she could not take the pain away from me but I drew great comfort from her being there with me. That is how it is with God and us in our time of darkness. God allows us the time it takes to learn, to grow, to heal from our darkness. At the same time, God never leaves us alone. We can count on this Compassionate Presence to be with us.

I have found remarkable comfort in knowing that God is a steadfast, compassionate Presence who will never leave me. Many years ago, a psalmist who must have known first-hand the terrors of the darkness, wrote this verse: "In the shadow of your wings I take refuge until the destruction is past" (Ps 57:l).[18] Taking shelter in the shadow of God's wings won't take away the darkness but it can ease the fear of the length or the intensity of it.

The woman at the retreat who described her relationship with God as "separate bedrooms" did have a consoling moment during those five days. It was on the day that we listened to a song by Colleen Fulmer titled "Rock Me Gentle."[19] The refrain pictures us being rocked in the arms of God as a child would be tenderly rocked in the arms of a loving parent. This woman came to me afterward with tears on her cheeks and whispered: "That's what I need—oh, yes—to just be held by God."

Knowing this truth of God's nearness does not keep us from all those natural consequences of the spiritual journey that I have described. We may be rocked and cradled in the arms of Compassion but we still have to face the painful terms of transformation. I continue to want a cozy, loving God who helps me to escape the difficult stages of transformation rather than a God who leaves me empty and who refuses to rescue me from my darkness until I've learned from it. In other words, there is simply no way to get out of the tough stuff of growth, no matter how intimate, deep and strong our relationship with God is. There has to be a real "dying" internally in order for new life to come forth.

What do we do, then, when we are experiencing the bleak land of darkness in our spiritual life? Besides striving to accept the darkness as a part of our growth, fidelity is so important. We need to keep crying out to God, bringing our tired, empty selves to this Sacred Source of Love. We need to let our feelings just be there and not give up on the journey. The Light never goes out for us, it is only hidden by the clouds of our present situation. God is just as present to us in our dark times as in our well-lighted ones. We ought not give up on God and on prayer at the time when we are most in need of this relationship.

It can be helpful, sometimes, to try new forms of prayer. This, too, might be part of the new life which awaits us. It may entail trying a very different way of daily relating to the Hidden One. I've known people who've walked or danced their way through the dark times. Others have used clay or paints or musical instruments or comforting music to stay connected with the Inner Presence whom they cannot feel.

Yes, and some cry their way through the dark times. Allowing our tears and our sorrow to fill our prayertime is another way to bring all that we are to the One who loves us tenderly and completely. It really does not make any difference what the form of prayer is. The important thing is that we make the effort to stay connected with our God. God understands our efforts and welcomes us as we are.

Sometimes we can gain courage in our present dryness by returning in memory to the past when we experienced emptiness and discouragement in our prayer. We can look back and see what we learned from that difficult time. How did that time shape and affect who we are today? What was the wisdom that was given to us? Our relationship with God needs to be nourished. The fire in us that has barely a glint of flame needs to be fed. This can be done in many ways: reading books that call to our hearts, listening to music that touches our soul, spending time with the earth or with understanding loved ones, exercising our body, or going to an energizing play or film. We may feel as if we are dragging ourselves to these activities, but in doing so we are silently proclaiming a belief that the fire has not gone out and that we are still willing to tend it. The Divine Light is not limited to being, present only in formal worship or personal prayer. God's love permeates our whole being, and thus we must tend to the various dimensions of who we are even when we feel too weary or dismal inside to care about anything.

I appreciate the Hebrew Scriptures for their honesty about God and the darkness which we humans experience. People are allowed to cry out their pain and their woe. This darkness is not denied but there is always the assurance that this will pass in time and that a happier phase of life will eventually come. Psalm 13 is a good example of this:

> How long, Yahweh, will you forget me? For ever?
> How long will you turn your face from me?
> How long must I nurse rebellion in my soul,
> sorrow in my heart day and night?
>
> As for me, I trust in your faithful love....
> Let my heart delight in your saving help,
> let me sing to Yahweh for (Yahweh's) generosity
>   to me,
> let me sing to the name of Yahweh ...[20]

We need to keep the spark of hope alive in us and cry out to God from the empty places of our hearts. What feels like "separate bedrooms" to us is only that: *a feeling*. In the deepest center of our soul the Divine Presence is there, rocking us gently, urging us to believe in the value of the dark dimensions of our journey.

Prayer

O God,
after all the time we've spent together,
I never thought it would come to this—
an immense chasm carved between us,
holding the empty echoes of my prayer.

All that remains of my worn out cries
is a tiny voice that longs for you.

Where are you, God, when I need you most?
Why won't you fix my life for me?
I need you to get me out of this darkness.
I demand that you give me extended bliss.

But my demands and my desires go unheeded
and all I hear is a tender Voice
whispering repeatedly: "I am with you."

–Joyce Rupp

Chapter Five
The Morning Will Come

I will keep still and wait like the night with starry vigil and its head bent low with patience.... The morning will surely come, the darkness will vanish....[21]

—*Rabindranath Tagore*

How different the night is when the skies are clear and filled with the radiance of a zillion stars than when the night is cloudy, humid, and filled with the rumblings of an approaching storm. Our inner darkness is no different. It seems to me that the stormy, rumbling night sky is like all those days, months (years, perhaps), when we are overwhelmed with our inner turmoil or emptiness. The radiant, star-filled night is like the remarkable and treasurable experience of someone bringing one's inner starlight into our lives. We need the night-time in order to see those stars just as we need our soul's night to fully appreciate the power of the inner light. When we glimpse the stars in our inner darkness we find strength and courage to go on.

The stars, those beautiful pieces of the Universe's light, have always been very comforting for me. When I walk under the stars I feel wrapped in the womb of the night, nurtured, tended to, loved. I always yearn to walk in the night but am usually too fearful to do so by myself. In the summer I celebrated my fiftieth birthday I decided to go camping alone in the Sangre de Cristo mountains. I knew I'd have some fear of the night but I also knew that I needed to ritualize this significant transition in my life. I'll never forget how I awoke that night and saw a brilliant light shining, casting shadows of all the tree branches on my tent. I thought that it was morning in the forest, but when I looked outside, I was absolutely astounded to see a full moon penetrating the darkness of the mountain. I got up and walked out into the night of which I had been afraid. To my surprise, I felt no fear at all. Instead, I felt a presence blessing me. I sensed a kinship with all the creatures of the mountain and with all of humanity. I stood and stood in the moonlight and felt an overwhelmingly kind radiance surround my heart. The night was still night. The darkness was still there but the moonlight took away all my resistance to it.

C. G. Jung wrote that from the soul's "primordial beginnings there has been a desire for light and an irrepressible urge to rise out of the primal darkness."[22] Accepting the darkness but also longing for the light is an immense paradox of our soul's journey. There will always be a part of us that yearns for the light when we are in the valley of gloom. This is our gift of hope. We need to go on believing, especially when we are deep in the tomb of darkness, that there is a welcoming light deep inside that is waiting for us.

I never cease to be amazed at the countless and surprising ways in which the light gradually comes and takes over the darkness which we have experienced. Even the smallest glimmer of light can be a strong and vibrant call of hope to our hearts. Have you ever noticed how a tiny candle can break the blackness of a dark room? The same is true for those many little pieces of light which illuminate the dark room of our hearts. Gary Zukov believes that "a soul with no light will always come to know Light because there is so much assistance provided to each soul at all times."[23] He is referring to the inner and outer guides and teachers who come unexpectedly into our lives and help to direct us toward wisdom.

Actually, this assistance comes to us in many ways. Each of us has a brilliant light within us—it is the Divine Illumination of our soul. This light carries an immense energy of love and wisdom and each of us bears this light every day of our lives even when the darkness looms so large that no light can be seen or felt. No wonder that Jesus referred to himself as "the Light," that he also spoke of us having light within us, and that he encouraged us to share this light with all (Jn 8:12; Mt 5:14-16).

"Light" can have a variety of meanings for people depending upon their beliefs and their life experience. For me, the light means all of these things: the divine presence within my being, the spark of my soul, the aura of energy I have within and around me, and the luminous energy that connects every part of the universe. My inner light bears a resemblance to the outer light of the sun in numerous ways. Just as the sun draws forth growth and ripens fruit, warms and comforts, and gives a greater clarity to the beauty of life, so, too, the many-faceted light that fills my being.

I have a good friend named Dorothy who has been blind for many years. When I am with her I never think of her blindness because so much light radiates from her presence. She once said to me, "I think that we are all little pieces of light for one another." That comment reached deeply into my memory because I instantly recalled so many people who had been there for me at just the time I needed them. They were a tiny spark of light and brought me hope when my night sky was very cloudy and stormy. I know that this is true for numerous people. So often I hear comments from retreatants who say that they never could have made it through the tough times had it not been for those who stood by them, kept on believing in them, and offered them comfort and support.

Sometimes just the memory of another's light can support and sustain us. I was never so aware of this as

when I participated in a Roman Catholic Mass on the feast of All Saints. The Mass was in a small church in a poor part of the city. Mostly children from a nearby inner city elementary school were present at the liturgy. The celebrant asked us to recall loved ones who had died during the past year and to think of these persons on the other side of life as beings who were now completely filled with light, illuminated with the goodness of "saints."

He then invited all the children who had experienced a loved one's death during the past year to come forward and receive a lit candle in honor of the person who had died. As several dozen children walked forward I was surprised at how many of them had been touched by death. As each child received the light and carried it to the altar, each told whom the light honored: "my brother, my sister, my dad, my grandmother…"

Tears filled my eyes as more and more lights sparkled and twinkled upon the altar. I felt the presence of the ancestors, "the wise ones," the souls who have a "knowing" we've yet to discover. I felt the strength of their presence and the power of their goodness. I thought, "If only they could speak to us, how much they would tell us about darkness and light!" It was a comforting time of memory for me as I, too, gathered all the saints I had known and received their sustaining and strengthening light into my heart.

Remembering the light-filled people we have known helps us to keep in mind how one person's inner light can make a significant difference in the lives of many people. When the fighting was fierce in Bosnia-Herzegovina, a general from France stood his ground and insisted that the besieged victims be evacuated. Nearly 700 were moved to safety because of his compassion and care. He allowed not just the sick and wounded to be moved but also their relatives. When this man was interviewed about his decision, he spoke of the pain and suffering he had seen. I noticed that his eyes held a deep and luminous compassion. It was this light that gave him the courage to reach out to those in the depths of despair. This person's "little piece of light" penetrated the darkness of war and brought freedom and hope to many hearts.

I've experienced some of the strongest light coming from those who've suffered the greatest darkness. It is as though the darkness forced them to be more open, vulnerable, needy, understanding. As this happened, their walls and defenses, their tightly held securities, fell away and the radiance within had so much more room to shine. In this way, we "find" our light. It's not just a matter of choosing to let our light shine; it also naturally happens when we are open and responsive to all of life. Stephen Mitchell acknowledges: "Before we can share the light, we have to find it. When we embody it, we can't help sharing it, because it has no limits."[24]

Sometimes it is not a direct encounter with a person whose light is shining that blesses us with hope. It can be a word or a smile or a card thoughtfully sent. The author of *The Power of One* expresses it this way:

Sometimes the slightest things clearly change the direction of our lives, the merest breath of circumstance, a random moment that connects like a meteorite striking the earth. Lives have survived and changed direction on the strength of a chance remark.[25]

I recall a minister who had been experiencing long bouts of depression because of the seeming lack of success in his parish. One day he went to visit a woman who was very ill. As he started to leave the room, the woman spoke to him: "You have been such an important person in my life. I want you to know that I have great love for you." These kind words sailed straight into the minister's heart. He told me that he just couldn't believe it but by the time he reached his office he could sense that something different was stirring within him. During the next several weeks the depression lifted and he felt a tremendous rejuvenation in his life.

The quickness with which the minister's darkness left is quite unusual. Normally, the dissipation of our internal darkness is much like the dawning of a new day. The sun rarely comes bursting up from the horizon immediately. Usually there is the first hint of light, then the changing coloration of the clouds, and finally the fullness of the sunshine upon the land. Something in us wants the light to be there instantly. Patience is the major virtue needed when we are in the bleak land of darkness. Not long ago, a friend of mine was speaking to me about his process of being in therapy. He said to me: "I wonder if I'm trying to hurry the process. I think I'm not being patient enough. It's hard not to be healthy immediately." How true this is!

It is also not unusual for those who've been in deep depression or sorrow for a long time to doubt the light when the first rays do begin to lift up onto the inner horizon. When light does come, there is hesitation, doubt, confusion, questions. There has been sorrow, sadness, emptiness, anger, for so long, how could it be that this is actually ending? Little voices from the pessimistic or doubtful part of self respond to the first rays of glimpsed light: "Oh, this won't last...I can't afford to believe that I may be feeling good again...I don't want to be disappointed...I must be imagining this...maybe there's something wrong with me, I'm beginning to feel happy again."

I've seen this same hesitancy as newly hatched butterflies are given their freedom. They don't immediately fly away. Oftentimes the butterflies will sit for quite a long time before they stretch their colored wings and lift off toward a flower or a twig. Sometimes they are waiting for their wings to get strong enough to fly—the blood of their birthing may need to be more fully circulated in their wings—and sometimes they are not quite dry enough. Other times it appears that they simply do not realize that they are actually free to go wherever they choose.

One of my favorite stories is about a woman who was working in a country where there were numerous rainbows every day. She had often expressed the wish that someday she could go stand in a rainbow. One day as she and her companions were driving along, they saw a magnificent rainbow a mile or so in front of them. She was elated and hurried to go and stand in it. When they arrived at the rainbow, the woman jumped out of the car and ran over to it. To her surprise, she couldn't tell when she was in the rainbow. She kept calling to the others, "Am I in it yet? Am I in it now?" "Yes, yes," they called back. "You're in it right now. You just can't see it, but we can."

The Light may be encompassing us but something about our inner terrain or our long bout with darkness may keep us from being able to see it or to accept it. We simply have to trust that it is so. It helps if we have others around us to assure us that we really are "standing in the light." Many times they can see this light from their perspective of life while we cannot do so from ours.

This hesitancy or lack of belief that the light is actually there reminds me of one of the beautiful Easter stories. Mary has gone to the tomb to anoint the dead body of Jesus. It is still dark on the first day of the week. She stands in the darkness. The tomb is open! She expects to find death there in the darkness but it is not there. She becomes confused. Where is the body? The doubtful or not-yet-wise part of her self concludes that someone must have taken or stolen it. She does not comprehend yet that Jesus has been raised from the dead. Mary cannot yet perceive that the light has overcome the darkness.

Mary runs and tells others that the body has been taken away. Later, when the dawn is upon the land,

Mary goes back to that empty place. She gathers up her courage and through her tears she peers into the darkness of the tomb. This time she sees two messengers of God. Before they can answer her question of where the body of Jesus has been taken, she turns around and sees the Risen Jesus in the garden. Mary still does not comprehend the power of the light. She thinks Jesus is a gardener. Only when he speaks does the truth of the resurrection finally penetrate Mary's awareness. She has been so over-whelmed with the darkness of his death and her sadness that this radical transformation of new life has been sim-ply incomprehensible to her. The sound of her name being called by her Beloved, who is "the Light," brings her out of her confusion (Jn 20 : 1-18).

We need to peer into the tomb of our own dark-ness. We must look back at our previous experiences of darkness, however large or small they might be, peer into those tomb-like inner travels, and discover what is and is not there. If we do not peer into our own inner tombs, we may just assume that there's still something dead in there. This peering into the tomb can be a strong source of hope for us as we see how our own resurrections have happened, what we have learned, how we have grown, and how the light has taken over our darkness. As we peer into that old, dark space, we may be surprised to dis-cover that this "dead" part of ourselves has fled the tomb and that we can more freely come forth into the garden of life.

Prayer

O God,
as I look back at my life
I see many little pieces of light.
They have given me hope and comfort
in my bleak and weary times.

I thank you for the radiance
of a dark sky full of stars,
and for the faithful light of dawn
which follows every turn of darkness.

I thank you for loved ones and strangers
whose inner beacons of light
have warmed and welcomed my pain.

I thank you for your Presence in my depths,
protecting, guiding, reassuring, loving.

I thank you for all those life-surprises
which sparked a bit of hope in my ashes.

And, yes, I thank you for my darkness,
(the unwanted companion I shun and avoid)
because this pushy intruder comes with truth
and reveals my hidden treasures to me.

—Joyce Rupp

Epilogue

*I*n The Heart of the Hunter, *Laurens van der Post describes a poignant scene in the midst of the Kalahari desert. He* is camped there with local bushmen and they are sitting around a campfire. The absence of any artificial light allows for a world of complete darkness once one moves beyond the campfire. The stars hang low in the sky, their brilliance not only seen but heard. Laurens van der Post describes the sound of the stars as "this intense electric murmur at one's ears." Then he sees the outline of a bushwoman holding her young infant up to the stars.

She is singing some kind of chant and has her face lifted to the sky.

When van der Post asked the local bushmen what the woman was doing, he was told that she was asking the stars to take the heart of her child and to give him "something of the heart of a star in return...because the stars have heart in plenty...." The heart of the stars is a hunting heart, one that seeks with courage and finds the nourishment which is needed for life.[26] When I read this explanation, I thought of all of us who have been in darkness. I thought of our own hearts and how, when we are gradually coming back to light, it is as though we have a "child" within us coming to birth.

This "child" may be a new way of living or loving, a deepened sense of self-esteem, a turning over of our old ways, a ripening of our ideas or beliefs, a wisdom that has come from our grieving, or any other thing that is fresh and new for us. If only we could, as the bushwoman did, take this "child" within us trustingly and hold it in our open hands. We could lovingly hold up whatever is waiting to be born in us, asking that this newness within us be blessed with the heart of the stars. We could pray that we receive a "hunting heart" so that we seek with courage and live with trust, believing that what we need for our soul will be given.

We carry our greatest treasure within us: a piece of light which will forever shine, a radiance which is always lighting our way home. Let us trust this light. It will never go out.

Notes

1. *The New Jerusalem Bible*, New York: Doubleday, 1985.

2. *Care of the Soul*, Thomas Moore. New York: HarperCollins Publ., 1992, p. 21.

3. *The Fruitful Darkness*, Joan Halifax. San Francisco: Harper SanFrancisco, 1993, p. 179.

4. *When the Heart Waits*, Sue Monk Kidd. San Francisco: Harper and Row, p. 152.

5. *The Power of One*, Bryce Courtenay. New York: Ballantine Books, 1991, p. 47.

6. *When a Child Dies*, Carol Pregent. Notre Dame: Ave Maria Press, 1992, p. 59.

7. *Healing into Life and Death*, Stephen Levine. New York: Doubleday Anchor Books, 1987, p. 222.

8. "My Fight for Justice," Robbi Sommers. *Reader's Digest*, April, 1993.

9. *The Holy Bible, New Revised Standard Version*, Nashville: Cokesbury, 1990.

10. *Gitanjali*, Rabindranath Tagore. New York: Macmillan Publ. Co., 1913, # 99, p. 111.

11. *The Moon and the Virgin*, Nor Hall. San Francisco: Harper and Row, 1980, p. 223.

12. *Transitions*, William Bridges. Reading, MA: Addison Wesley Publ. Co., 1980, p. 117.

13. *The Heroine's Journey*, Maureen Murdock. Boston: Shambhala, 1990, p. 88.

14. *A Tree Full of Angels*, Macrina Wiederkehr. San Francisco: Harper and Row, 1988, p. 46.

15. *Gift of the Dark Angel*, Ann Keiffer. San Diego: LuraMedia Publ., 1991, p. 114.

16. As quoted in *A Path with Heart*, Jack Kornfield. New York: Doubleday Bantam Books, 1993, p. 100.

17. *When the Heart Waits*, Sue Monk Kidd. San Francisco: Harper and Row, 1990, p. 146.

18. *The New Jerusalem Bible*, New York: Doubleday, 1985.

19. *Her Wings Unfurled*, Colleen Fulmer (cassette tape, 1989). Loretto Spirituality Network, 725 Calhoun St., Albany, CA 94706.

20. *The New Jerusalem Bible* New York: Doubleday, 1985.

21. *Gitanjali*, Rabindranath Tagore. New York: Macmillan Publ. Co., 1913, # 19, p. 37.

22. *Memories, Dreams, Reflections*, C. G. Jung. New York: Random House, 1961, p. 269.

23. *The Seat of the Soul*, Gary Zukov. New York: Simon & Schuster, 1989, p. 71.

24. *The Gospel According to Jesus*, Stephen Mitchell. New York: HarperCollins Publ., 1991, p. 161.

25. *The Power of One*, Bryce Courtenay. New York: Ballantine Books, 1989, p. 62.

26. *The Heart of the Hunter*, Laurens van der Post. New York: Wm. Morrow & Co., 1961, pp. 32-33.